I0838067

THE BORED PHOTOGRAPHER

STEFANO BROLI

CONTENTS

PREFACE

Have you ever been in a situation where you once loved doing something so much, but now you can't find the same level of passion? Perhaps you've become bored or disillusioned and are now struggling to regain the spark that once fueled your passion. This is the dilemma that I seek to address throughout this book.

Photography captures the essence of life. It's a medium that can take you on a journey and allow you to see the world in a different light – colours, shapes, and lighting all impact the feeling you evoke in an audience. But what happens when the passion that once drove you to take photos fades away? In the age of smartphones and social media, we are all, in one way or another, photographers. Yet, with more and more content being published every day, naturally, you may be finding yourself uninspired. How can I possibly stand out from the crowd, when the crowd has grown exponentially? This is where this book can come in and provide the help you are seeking.

As a photographer, I capture the world through my lens. I may be exploring the streets and alleys of my city, working on a personal project, or taking portraits of friends and family. No matter what project I am taking on, photography is a creative outlet, one that offers a way to refuel my mind with positive energy. In fact, photography is sometimes seen as a lonely experience; yet, I feel it is anything but. In fact, I constantly work with incredible artists, and one by one, they each fuel my creative outlet each in their own way. This is how I fuel my creativity, but your fuel may be different. This book is about rediscovering your passion and reconnecting with why you chose to pursue your chosen profession. I know what feeling lost and unmotivated is like having been there a few times already. Trust me when I say that it's possible to reignite this creativity..

"The Bored Photographer" is not just about photography, but about getting you to feel passionate again. I want you to find the passion and creativity that first got you interested in photography in the first place again! So, it's about understanding why you got into the field in the first place and discovering new ways to find joy and satisfaction in your work.

INTRODUCTION

efore we get started, let's make this clear: this is not a photography manual or a step by step guide on how to take better photos. This is about getting your 'mojo' back! There's a grey space that I often visit, and so do many friends and photographers I know, for many reasons: the space of dullness, when finding any kind of motivation is difficult. I want to help you get out of this funk.

When you run a photography business or when you work a 'normal' job, your 9-5 responsibilities come first, and it's not just the lack of time that stops you. It's that simple question that seeds in your mind, saying, "Why waste your time?".

Deepak Chopra once said "Always go with your passions. Never ask yourself if it's realistic or not." But what happens when reality sets in? What happens when things don't go as planned or your passion cannot feed the reality- or feed you! Do you start to lose interest in that childhood dream, or do you find a way to make it work despite all the challenges it poses?

I am a lover of photography. I wake up every morning with a bright smile, ready to put that same smile on somebody through my photography. You can tell from afar that I love what I do. I spend hours taking pictures, editing them, and sharing them online. Photography is my passion, and I have always dreamt of becoming a renowned photographer. That being said, despite my love for photography, do you really think that every morning, I wake up feeling like Harry Potter after he defeated Voldemort? Of course not – we all have 'bad' days.

You don't start doubting yourself and your passion all of a sudden. It is a compilation of little changes that have been occurring around you that you refuse to take note of. Life circumstances can profoundly impact your choices and decisions, and hence, can change how passionate or creative you feel on a certain day. Whether it is financial instability, family responsibilities, health issues, or other other kinds of factors, the challenges you face daily will without a doubt affect how you feel about your work on any given day. We are human beings after all!

But that doesn't mean that you are the victim of your circumstances. There are ways around feeling like this and losing all passion. How? This is what this book teaches you! Let's get started.

DON'T BOTHER THE CAMERA

Before we dive into the details, we need to start with the groundwork. A camera is just an interface to see the world. It's the eye that makes the photograph. You're not judged by the quality of your gear, but by the way you see the world. The camera does not create the photograph itself, we do. We see the world a certain way and capture that vision through the lens. The quality of our gear may affect the technical features of the image, but ultimately, our imagination and creativity is what make the photograph unique.

Photography is more than just taking pictures. It's the alignment of your feelings, experiences, and ideas in relation to a particular moment. A camera is only a *tool* that can help you to capture the world around you, it is an instrument that can help you express yourself. The camera is an **instrument** that can help you to explore and interpret the world around you. When you pick up a camera, you are not just taking a snapshot of what is in front of you but also **interpreting what you see**. The camera can help you see things you might not have noticed before, or see things in a new way.

When you take a photo, you capture not just an image but also a moment in time, a feeling, or an emotion elaborated through your own personal experiences and feelings, making that picture unique. Using your camera as a way of expression means that you not only take photos of what is right in front of you, but also capture your *own perspective and feelings*. You can experiment with different angles, lighting, and compositions to convey the mood and emotion you want to express, and you can also use editing tools to enhance or transform your images, creating something that is uniquely yours.

However, to be able to express yourself through photography, you need to have the right **mindset**. You need to have an open mind and a curious spirit so you can see the world around you with fresh eyes and to find beauty in unexpected places. You must also be patient and persistent to keep practising and learning from your mistakes. Photography is a process of trial and error, and it takes time and effort to master. You need to be willing to experiment, take risks, and push yourself out of your comfort zone.

When we view the world and our passions from our *own* perspective, we identify what resonates with us, what we value most, and what inspires us. We embrace our perspective and bring fresh and innovative ideas that become groundbreaking

– the pictures that emerge from this mindset truly become works of art. Our unique experiences, and especially our ability to dive into this mindset, can lead to new solutions to this dullness we are experiencing, to creative approaches, and exciting opportunities that may not have been explored yet. Sometimes, all we need is a kick that allows us to see things differently.

Each photographer has their own style, approach, and vision when capturing an image. The camera and equipment you choose to use are tools that allow you to express yourself and your creativity. Whether you prefer the versatility of a digital camera or the nostalgic feel of an analogue film camera, your choice of equipment should reflect your personal preferences and needs as a photographer. The same goes for the lenses you choose, which can greatly affect your photos' composition, depth, and mood.

When you choose a camera, you choose a tool that can help you express yourself. Some photographers prefer to use film cameras because they like the texture and feel of the film. Others prefer digital cameras because of the convenience and flexibility they offer. Whatever camera brand you choose, it should be one that you feel comfortable using and allows you to express yourself in the way you want to. Some photographers prefer to shoot in black and white because they feel it adds a timeless and classic quality to their images. Others prefer to shoot in vibrant colours to capture the energy and vitality of the world around them. Whatever colours you choose, that is up to you. Just you.

You should not worry about whether you are a professional or an amateur photographer. You should not worry about competing with others or meeting a certain standard. Instead, you should focus on rediscovering the world, seeing it through your own eyes, and expressing your *unique* perspective. Photography is **not** a competition, and you do not need to measure your skills or success against anyone else's. Social media and online platforms can sometimes create an unhealthy environment of comparison and pressure, but **staying true to yourself and your artistic vision is essential.**

BE YOURSELF

In today's world, it's easy to get caught up in the hustle and bustle of daily life, and sometimes it feels like we're expected to conform to certain standards or fit into a particular mould. This is especially true when we consider the world of photography!

As human beings, we have an innate desire to explore and discover the world around us. Whether through travel, art, or personal relationships, we seek to understand the world and our place in it.

As photographers, we often discover the world through photography. When doing so, **start with what you know best**. Whether it's a favourite place, a treasured object, or a beloved friend or family member, we all have things in our lives that we feel a strong connection to. We can tap into a deep well of inspiration and meaning by using these as a starting point for our creative exploration. Find something that triggers all sorts of emotions within you and listen to your gut – the resulting pictures are often some of the most powerful ones we take.

It's not always easy to tap into our creativity and rediscover the world around us. Sometimes, we might feel stuck or unsure of where to start. If this is the case, try **simplifying things and focusing on the basics**. Take a step back and focus on the essential elements of your photography. Don't get into your head – just take pictures.

Other than you, no one else genuinely understands what makes you need to be happy. Realising this is crucial because it prevents you from continuously attempting to appease other people, which is a surefire way never to be able to be satisfied with your own work. So, look for ways to be happy yourself.

See yourself as someone who has something to say, and say it **through photography**. Shoot the way you feel without asking yourself why. For example, you can start with your emotions. What do your emotions drive you towards? How do you feel about certain places, people, objects, or events? You only need to take the first step in the right direction. This is all about curiosity! Be confident about this curiosity and start taking photos.

For example, I personally use a Leica Q2 because I realised that I mostly shoot street-photography and candid photography. I switch off the digital screen, don't review unless necessary, and sometimes shoot without seeing through the viewfinder. I like to focus just on the moments and not the photo I captured already. I make sure that when I do shoot something, I do it for myself. I want the result to be something that *I* am happy with, and something that represents the vision that *I* have for this project, not to make sure that the algorithm is happy with my photograph!

Sometimes, less is more. This is something I've had to learn throughout my years of experience. While you might try to think about all the details, the different lenses, the different views and highlights and lighting and colours around you, it might very well be easier to simply focus on what you see right in front of your eyes. Think less so you can think more. This may sound counterintuitive or may even sound like it makes very little sense, but think about it: the more you think, the more you get in your head. Then, the more you are in your head, the less you can truly focus on what's in front of you and what you want to capture. So, stop getting in your head and just hit *click*.

The goal is to shoot *for yourself,* not for the likes, the followers, or the algorithm. Let your talent shine through!

THE NATIONAL GALLERY
FREE ADMISSION
NATIONAL GALLERY

DON'T TAKE THE BUS

Photography is not about you not listening to other people's opinions on your life, but about being true to yourself. It is not about you doing the same comfortable process over and over again and expecting a different result each time. Instead, challenge yourself: take the longest route and enjoy the little things you see on the way.

Sticking to our comfort zone may feel safe and secure, but it can also lead to boredom and complacency, especially when it comes to creative work like photography. When we limit ourselves to what we already know and are comfortable with, we miss out on the opportunities for growth and exploration that come with stepping outside our comfort zone. Instead, putting ourselves in uncomfortable positions is what drives us to try out different things, and often, the best pictures come out from such instances.

As a photographer, seeing the world with fresh eyes is important. You can't create truly compelling images without paying attention to the details and nuances of the world around you. Seeing the world, people, things, light, colours, and weather is crucial for building your vision and developing your photography skills. For this, take the long road. Enjoy the little things you see on the way. Start walking, and don't go the easy way. Force uncomfortable decisions, keeping in mind the long term goal which is to take the best photographs you've taken in a long time.

In fact, one of the keys to seeing the world in a new way is to become a **spectator**. Instead of rushing from place to place, take the time to observe your surroundings. Walk slowly and deliberately, taking in everything around you. Look up, down, and around, paying attention to the small and big picture details. As you walk, **expand your senses**. Listen to the sounds of the world around you. Feel the textures of different surfaces. Smell the scents in the air. Taste the flavours of the food and drinks you consume. All of these sensory experiences can help you to see the world in a more vibrant and nuanced way. Pay attention to the people you encounter as you walk. Notice their expressions, body language, and interactions with their surroundings. These observations can help you to create more compelling images of people in their environment.

Light and colour are also incredibly important in photography. As you walk, pay attention to how the light changes throughout the day. Notice how it interacts with different surfaces and objects, creating shadows, reflections, and highlights. Look for interesting colour combinations and how they change in different lighting situations. These observations can help you to create images that capture the essence of a place or moment.

As someone who loves taking photographs, I know how rain, snow, fog, and other weather conditions can dramatically alter the scenery and transform the images you capture. Rather than being intimidated by these elements, embrace them and use them to your advantage. They have the power to add depth and character to your photos, making them even more memorable and captivating.

These observations and experiences can help you build your vision as a photographer. They can inspire you to see the world in new ways and create unique and meaningful images. But building your vision isn't just about seeing things in a new way – **it's also about understanding your own perspective and how you relate to the world around you.**

As you walk and observe, take note of your own thoughts and emotions. What do you feel as you take in your surroundings? What captures your attention and why? How do you want to convey these emotions in your art?

By walking instead of taking a bus or other transportation (metaphorically-speaking), you're allowing yourself to see things differently. You can move at your *own* pace, stopping to take in the details and elements that catch your eye, instead of only being focused on the destination. This is how you can create more interesting and unique photographs that truly capture the essence of the place you're exploring.

Walking forces you to *slow down* and pay attention to what's happening around you, which is something we struggle to do in this day and age! The key is to approach your photography with intention and purpose, and for this, you need to slow down. Rather than simply snapping pictures and hoping for the best, take the time to think about what you're trying to capture and why. What story do you want your images to tell? **What emotions do you want to convey?** Be intentional.

The more experience you gain as a photographer, the more you will learn about your style, what you enjoy shooting, and the world of possibilities you have in terms of what you can shoot. So, don't take the bus, but walk it out – you will get to see a lot more than what you *would* see if you were to only get to the destination. The goal is not to jump through the steps quickly so you can only photograph the final destination, but to take in the beauty around you and to see potential in all the landscapes (metaphorically-speaking or not) around. You might find a diamond in the rough while walking there. Get the longest route and enjoy the little things you see on the way.

Likewise, you want to force uncomfortable decisions, having in mind a long-term goal. Nothing worth having will come perfectly easily to you, which means that you need to push your own boundaries to find new things to shoot and to get the best results.

On the other hand, you also want to limit yourself to be free. In other words, instead of trying to shoot absolutely everything you see, you want to limit this to what you *truly* enjoy.

Finally, don't be shy and feel like the main character of a story that walks, observing the world in its beauty. You never know what you might come across on one of your walks, and life is too short to act as though we are nonchalant about the beauty surrounding us. Be the main character, feel like one, and click!

BE A PUNK!

In your attempt to be a perfectionist in everything you do, you end up forgetting what it is like to enjoy the process, the delays, and the little emotional setbacks that happen to you on your road to achieving your dream. You can never be perfect at the job, skill or passion, but you can continually improve every day to be sure you are better than yesterday. Be in competition with yourself and not with anyone else!

Do what you like with consciousness by being aware of why you are doing what you are doing and ensuring it aligns with your values and passion. This means being *present* and fully *engaged* in the activity instead of going through the motions without much thought. It also means *approaching the activity with intention*. You are clear on why you are doing it and what you hope to gain from it.

The action of taking a photograph is easy – you just press a button. The real work is finding the creativity to take a photograph that aligns with the vision you have. Sometimes, that means that you need to break a few rules! For example, you can start by ignoring conventional wisdom and experimenting with new techniques and approaches. Push the boundaries and establish your unique style and voice within the masses of photographers.

And yes, that means that sometimes, you just won't get the results you're after. But that's part of the deal too. When we constantly strive for perfection, we can become overly self-critical and anxious, two emotions we don't want when taking photographs. We can appreciate the small moments and find happiness in the journey instead of just focusing on success. Perfectionism hinders creativity in that it makes us rigid and inflexible in our thinking, limiting our ability to think outside the box.

So embrace the present moment and savour the experiences that make photography worthwhile. Go out of your way to break the rules, and live in the moment. Sure, you might not follow the current properly, but this is how you can create truly disruptive content! In fact, rules of composition and photography in general are important for a photographer but in this process of "rediscovering passion" can be left behind in favour of the instinct. In photography, we use "shoot from your gut" as opposed to "brain photography" – keep this in mind as you shoot!

So, respect the rules when it is needed, and break them when the risks aren't too high. For example, respect them when they are there to protect other people and their privacy, but break them when they don't make any sense or when they result in outcomes that are worth the risk. Do what you like with consciousness, always keeping respect in mind for the people involved in your photography. In fact, knowing the rules is just as important as not letting them interfere with the moment!

Besides this, focus on the moment and *not* on the technique. This is a big statement, and of course, it is easier to say than to apply, but once you start reacting to moments without thinking about the horizon, the rule of thirds, the Rembrandt's light... you'll be more connected with what is inside the photo. This is so you shoot *less* with your brain, and more with your gut, so you get butterflies again!

TAKE A STEP BACK

Photography is not just about clicking the perfect shot; it's about capturing the essence of the moment. And to capture that essence, a photographer must be patient and observant. They must wait and watch, studying the scene before them and anticipating the perfect moment to take the shot.

How often do we rush through our days, always hurrying to get to the next thing on our to-do list? We're so focused on where we're going that we forget to **appreciate the journey.** Waiting is a key element in photography – we need to wait to capture the perfect moment. As mentioned earlier, being a successful photographer is not just about having the latest gear or technical knowledge; it requires a keen eye for detail and especially an ability to **anticipate the perfect shot.**

In 2010, I took what has become my most famous photograph, "Only the Penitent Man," which was recognized by National Geographic and exhibited across Europe. This photograph resulted from careful observation and waiting for the perfect moment. I waited almost an hour on the Saint Malo fortified wall, anticipating the perfect shot. I had envisioned a person standing in front of the ocean waves, and I was determined to capture that moment. As I waited, I remained focused on my goal, taking in the scenery and observing the people around me. Finally, the moment I had been waiting for arrived. A person walked onto the wall and stood before the ocean waves, just as I had pictured. I quickly took the shot, and it became the iconic image that has earned recognition beyond what I could have ever expected. This experience is one that taught me patience. I know how to observe better, and I can now envision the perfect shot more successfully.

In photography, as in life, we must learn to see the world with fresh eyes. It's easy to get bogged down in the routine and familiarity of daily life, but by taking a step back and approaching the world with a fresh perspective, we can discover beauty and meaning in unexpected places. The world is full of wonder and awe, and by staying open and curious, we can capture the essence of the moment and create memories that will last a lifetime.

Have you ever noticed how a photographer can freeze a single moment in time and turn it into a powerful story with just one image? It's an incredible skill to have - waiting for that perfect moment to capture. You need to wait for the moment to come to you. Observation is learning and capturing life through the eyes before you turn to your camera. Your camera is an *extension* of your eye.

Wait for the extraordinary. For anything unusual that happens right in front of your camera. Wait for something that is worth you leaving your comfort zone. And then, *click*.

Finally, remember the "Master the Corner" concept in street photography. This refers to waiting, walking in circles, looking in every direction, and taking photos of just about anything that you find interesting happening in a specific location. This is one of the commandments of street photography!

Caution
Obstructing
the doors is
dangerous
and causes
delays

TAKE A STEP FORWARD

When it comes to photography, there's nothing more frustrating than missing the perfect shot because we hesitated or allowed our thoughts to get in the way. Whether it's because we're worried about what other people might think or we're second-guessing ourselves, allowing our thoughts to take over can be a real obstacle to achieving our goals as photographers. That's why it's so important to stay true to our vision and to be unapologetic in our pursuit of the "perfect" shot. Once we've identified the right moment to take a photo, we need to act and take the shot without hesitation. This means **putting aside doubts or fears and trusting our instincts and vision.**

However, in photography, as in many aspects of life, there is a delicate balance between being true to oneself and **respecting others.** It's important to identify the right moment to take a photo, but it's equally important to do so without causing any harm or offence to those around us. This often requires us to come out of our comfort zone, push ourselves beyond our usual limits and take **risks** to pursue our creative vision.

Whether you are trying a new technique, experimenting with different equipment or venturing into a new genre of photography, try to challenge yourself, especially if you are in a funk. In photography, as in life, it can be easy to fall into a comfortable routine. We may become used to taking the same types of pictures or following the same daily routines without venturing outside our comfort zone. But true growth and improvement only happen when we take risks and step out of that comfortable bubble and into the unknown.

You should also always "test the moment" and then come closer if you feel safe doing so and if the moment is still relevant. Try to *understand* the moment, so take a step back without interfering, if necessary.

Likewise, keep your photography simple, as mentioned before. Just take the risk! Respect people, don't be afraid to break the ice with strangers, and don't be afraid if someone asks you questions. People are curious. It's not every day that someone sees someone taking pictures of something that they themselves have most likely never noticed! So, if they ask, be friendly and empathise with people. They want to know more about your art, and they are interested in what you are doing. So, indulge them! Speak with them about what you are doing. Share it with them and bring people in – this is what art is all about!

FAIL TO SUCCEED

When it comes to photography, even the most experienced photographers will have works that don't turn out quite as planned. But even in these cases, there is often something to be learned or appreciated. For example, a blurry, overexposed or underexposed photo may reveal unexpected details that would make it worthy – and often, it might teach you what you can do differently next time! Even a photo with a finger in front of the lens can be a success if it captures a unique moment or emotion.

Consider the story of Thomas Edison, one of the most famous inventors of all time. Edison is best known for inventing the light bulb, but his road to success was far from smooth. Edison failed more than 10,000 times before finally creating a working light bulb. Instead of giving up, he viewed each failure as an opportunity to learn and improve. He famously said, *"I have not failed. I've just found 10,000 ways that won't work."* Apply this to your work. No, you haven't failed – you have only found something that doesn't work, which tells you what you need to change in the future for your pictures to work out the way you want them to.

In photography, mistakes are just as important as successes. Every photographer has taken photos that didn't turn out quite as planned, whether that's due to a technical error or a missed opportunity. But these mistakes can be valuable learning experiences. We can identify areas for improvement and refine our skills by analysing what went wrong – was the lens wrong? Did you wait too long? Did you wait until you'd have the perfect shot only to back out because you didn't feel confident? Don't judge yourself by the shots you missed. In fact, taking a nice photograph is much harder than taking a bad one, but the **more you fail, the more you are likely to succeed!**

Of course, it's not always easy to embrace failure. It can be difficult to admit when we've made a mistake and even harder to pick ourselves up and try again, especially if we *really* wanted that shot to be perfect. The key is to view failure not as a setback but as a stepping stone to success. No photographer becomes great overnight; it takes years of practice and experimentation to refine one's skills, but that's just it – you need practice. In photography, the more you practise, the better you identify and correct common mistakes.

But practising is not just about avoiding mistakes; it's also about developing a sense of intuition and spontaneity. When we practise something enough, it becomes second nature, and we can act quickly and decisively in the moment. In photography, this means being able to adjust camera settings on the fly or anticipating a shot before it happens. This is why starting small and building gradually is so important; it allows us to develop these skills and build our confidence over time.

Finally, you shouldn't build excessive expectations on the photos you are taking. This is because the reception might not be as good as you imagine. For example, chances are that you have taken photos in the past that you thought would be ground breaking, or that you were certain would gain great feedback, only for people barely to look at them or to respond at all. This is heartbreaking for any artist – you've put in all this work, only for people to barely notice it. Or, you have put in all this effort and time into a piece that you felt would change the game, and you are met with an underwhelming response. It's a difficult realisation to come to, hence why you should lower your expectations and remember the key in photography: shoot for **yourself**! If *you* are happy with the shoot, if *you* are happy with the outcome, then truly, that's all that matters. Don't let the reception stop you from trying again or from continuing your work as a photographer.

LEAVE THE UMBRELLA AT HOME

As children, we have all experienced the pure bliss of jumping in puddles of water, much to our parents' disapproval. While they worried about how they would get us back home without getting mud and dirt all over the car seats, we worried about one thing and one thing only: having fun. This concept can be applied to photography as well! Don't be afraid of getting wet and dirty and playing with the elements. Learn and re-discover the joy we used to feel as kids with things as simple as puddles and dirt. Don't just go the easy way – embrace transformation and focus only on the moments you spend in front of the camera.

Transformation is a powerful concept that can change how we see the world around us. Whether it's a physical transformation, like the changing weather, or a mental transformation, like a shift in perspective, transformation acts as a catalyst for growth and discovery. With photography, transformation happens when we appreciate our surroundings for all that they have to offer, and all the unique intricacies we may find by looking just a *bit* deeper.

When we think of transformation in photography, one of the first things that come to mind is the changing weather. Whether it's a sudden storm or a beautiful sunrise, the weather can transform a scene in a matter of moments. This can be a challenge, as it requires us to be adaptable and flexible, but it can also be an opportunity to capture something truly unique and memorable for your audience.

For example, a sudden downpour can turn an ordinary street scene into a stunning reflection of light and colour. How the rain interacts with the pavement and the surroundings can create a new perspective on an otherwise familiar scene. Embrace this transformation and see the world as a playground to capture beautiful and unexpected images!

But transformation isn't *just* about the weather. It's about seeing the world differently and being open to the unexpected. This can be particularly important in extraordinary circumstances, when our world may change in ways we could never have imagined.

Take the COVID-19 pandemic, for example. The pandemic has transformed the world in countless ways, from how we interact with each other to how we see ourselves and our place in the world. This has been an opportunity for photographers to rediscover the world around them, even in the most difficult and challenging circumstances. Photographers have captured powerful images of healthcare workers on the front lines of the pandemic, providing care and support to those who need it most. They have documented the empty streets and shuttered businesses that were once bustling with activity, which reminded us of the impact of the pandemic on our daily lives. We also captured images of the natural world as it continues to thrive and transform despite the chaos and uncertainty of the human world – the fish coming back to Venice, our skies being cleared of smog, and the list goes on. To see the world differently, we have to be willing to question everything we see and believe in, and sometimes, that starts with how we view our current situation, especially if it changes drastically like it did during Covid-19!

At the same time, it's important to remember that not every experiment will be a success. Sometimes we get rained on when things don't go according to plan – and we need to be ready to deal with being wet and dirty. But that's part of the learning process. Learn to adapt!

This is particularly relevant in the world of photography, where there are often many "rules" and conventions that are considered standard. But some of the most powerful images challenge these norms and break the rules to create something truly unique and memorable. It is a call to action, a reminder that we can do *so much more* than we often give ourselves credit for. We don't have to fear the unknown or take risks. We can embrace uncertainty and use it to fuel our creativity and passion.

At its core, photography is about more than just capturing a moment. It's about seeing the world in a new way and capturing that vision in a way that inspires others. Through it all, photographers have used transformation as an excuse to rediscover the world around them, even in extraordinary circumstances. This is how you create truly captivating images.

SALE
50% OFF
SALE
50% OFF

PREPARE THE SCENE

Composing a scene in photography is not a passive process. It requires active engagement with the environment and a deep understanding of the elements that make up the scene. Finding the balance between the elements in a photograph is how you can create a successful composition. Balance is achieved by carefully considering the placement of each element in the scene and their relationship to one another – the colours, the lighting, the sharp elements, and the like. **Every detail matters**, from the placement of objects in the scene to the lighting and shadows that create depth and contrast.

It is not enough to simply replicate the work of other photographers: to truly capture the world in every detail, you must bring your own unique perspective and style to the composition. Thinking back on how your photo should be and waiting for something to complete the scene is an important part of this creative process. It involves envisioning the final product before it even exists and actively working to bring that vision to life. It also needs you to have a willingness to wait for the right moment, light, or element to complete the scene. It's just like a painter's process – you see the pond before someone jumps in it. You see a wall with patterns of shadows that only needs a person to walk past. And then, you click – and there you have it, the perfect picture. Waiting for something to complete the scene can be frustrating, but it is essential to creating a compelling image. It might be waiting for a cloud to move or for the light to change. It might be waiting for a person to enter the frame or for a bird to take flight. Whatever it is, you must be patient and ready to capture the moment when it finally arrives.

Waiting for something to happen that matches your imagination can be both exciting and frustrating. On one hand, the anticipation of finding that missing piece can be thrilling. It is the hope that something incredible is on the horizon, just waiting to be discovered. However, on the other hand, the waiting can feel endless, like a never-ending journey without a clear destination.

The photo in your mind is a *representation* of your imagination. It is the *visual representation* of the idea that you hold. It could be a creative project you have been working on for months or years, or it may be something you've just been inspired to do. Whatever it is, the photo in your mind represents the potential for something great.

The missing piece in the photo is what you are waiting for. It could be a person, a ray or sun, or a sharp edge needed to make your idea a reality. Whatever it is, it is the *one thing* that will bring your imagination to life. The final puzzle piece will complete the picture and make it whole. It can be hard to stay motivated and focused when the end goal seems so far away. It is easy to get discouraged when things are not moving as quickly as you would like them to. Sometimes, the missing piece in the photo may not be what we expected. It may be something completely different, and we must recognize it when it presents itself. It may be a detour or a change in direction that leads us to where we need to be. It may be a new opportunity that we had not considered before.

However, remember that waiting is not *passive*. Waiting requires action and effort – and it takes a lot of effort to remain patient!

JUXTAPOSITION

"If you want to work for yourself, you have to know yourself first, and there's no better teacher of self-knowledge than self-employment." Peter Kozodoy

When we look at a photograph, we may initially see a collection of elements arranged in a particular way. However, the true power of photography lies in the ability to read these elements and make them discuss with each other to create new meanings. This is what is known as juxtaposition.

Juxtaposition involves placing two or more elements together to create a contrast or a connection. It can be used intentionally or unconsciously, but it always involves carefully considering the elements in the photograph and how they relate to each other. A picture of a child playing in a park may seem simple at first glance. However, by looking closely at the elements in the photograph, we see the potential for juxtaposition. Perhaps there is a group of adults in the background who are engaged in a serious conversation, creating a contrast between the child's carefree play and the adults' weighty concerns.

Juxtaposition is something that photographers do on autopilot. It is a way of expressing their unique perspective and capturing the essence of a moment in time. You read the elements in a photograph and make them discuss with each other, so you create a new and meaningful interpretation of the world around you.

The beauty of juxtaposition is that it can be used in various contexts, from street photography to photo-journalism to portraits. It is a versatile technique to convey various emotions and ideas through images. For this, you need to **read the elements in a photograph and understand how they relate to each other,** visualising the potential for juxtaposition before you take a picture.

For this, you will, once again, want to practise observing the world around you. Take the time to notice the way that different elements in a scene interact with each other. Pay attention to the emotions and ideas that are conveyed through these interactions.

For example, picking up from the previous chapter, juxtaposition is about reading the elements in a photo to make them discuss together and create new meanings. Try to pinpoint and play with opposites, similarities, colours, and textures. Create in-shot connections between different elements. These elements might trigger some questions when they are in connection, even if they are totally unrelated. So, read the moment. Act quickly and trust your eyes – you know best! In fact, this might be unconscious or intentional, but it will still happen, especially as you read the scene and observe what happens in front of your eyes. This is something a photographer does on *auto-pilot,* as the pilot is the true self and trusts oneself. This is a way of expression, a way of showing something unique and entirely irreplaceable. On a deeper scale, this is all about observations.

BLACK AND WHITE

Photography means "writing with light". The stronger the light, the stronger the shadow. When a photograph is taken, light enters the camera and is directed by lenses and mirrors to form an image on a light-sensitive surface, such as film or a digital sensor. The amount of light, direction and quality are all factors you can control to achieve the desired effect. In fact, the stronger the light, the stronger the shadow. With strong shadows, you can create surreal scenes when shooting. Specifically, black and white is not just a technique of photography. It's a form of expression that captures the world in its most basic form, devoid of colour, and brings out the details of light and shadow.

But beyond its technical aspects, black and white photography can also serve as a metaphor for how we see the world and live our lives. When we see the world in black and white, we are forced to focus on the essence of things, on the forms, lines, and textures. The absence of colour removes distractions and draws our attention to the contrasts and the tonal range. This is something you can apply to your photography: what features do you want to highlight?

Black and white photography can also evoke a sense of mood and emotion. The stark contrasts and tonal range can create a sense of drama, melancholy, or nostalgia. So, you can choose where to focus your attention: the light or the shadow. The way you do this can completely change the result of the photograph. If you focus on the light, you can create a bright, airy image. If you focus on the shadow, you can create a moody, dramatic image with a sense of mystery and depth. Each choice creates a different atmosphere and a different emotional response.

In fact, the darker the night, the brighter the light. Try to find highlights and use them to define specific shapes and moments that add to your photography. You might find street lights, low sunlight or cars to add to the shades and the lights. Ultimately, how you see the light and use it in your art defines who you are as a photographer.

STORYTELLING

A photograph has the power to evoke emotions, tell a story, and inspire people. To approach photography with a storyteller's eye is to create visually stunning images with a deeper meaning. This requires a conscious effort to understand the story **you** want to tell and pay attention to the technical aspects of photography.

Approaching photography with the eye of a storyteller is to understand the story you want to tell. For this, you have to have a clear vision of the message you want to convey through your images. Projects with multiple images, for example, are a way to showcase your point of view through linear storytelling.

One of the main advantages of creating multiple-image projects is that they enable you to experiment with different techniques, styles, and approaches. A project of multiple images, for example, can convey a story that words alone cannot express, revealing different aspects of your chosen theme or idea. This is how you can create a narrative that engages your audience and invites them to explore the images in-depth as well as the subject, whether it is a linear narration of an event or a conceptual project about the impact of climate-change. As a photographer, you are also an *author*, and your mission is to send your message to your destination.

Creating projects of multiple images is also an opportunity to see your production from an **external point of view**. When we create something, we risk being so focused on the process that we lose sight of the final product's essence. Viewing your production from an external point of view allows you to see your work as *others* see it, which gives you insights into what you are trying to express. You might have a clear idea of what you are trying to convey, but others might not if this is too 'internal'. Instead, viewing the project from an external point of view can help you see what is missing or what needs to be added to tell the story more effectively.

Once you have identified the story, you can work on creating images that capture the essence of your message. These images are frozen moments, but you are moving the narration one shutter click at a time. Be **conscious** of the story you want to tell, and approach it with the eye of a story-teller. This means thinking *beyond* the technical aspects of taking a photograph. It means considering the *narrative* behind the image and the emotions you want to evoke in your audience.

To effectively convey your message, it's important to fully understand *how* we see things. For example, know how our eyes perceive colour, contrast, and depth.

Ask yourself what kind of story you would like to tell, and do it like someone who *has something incredible to tell*. Think outside the box, but stay true to yourself. What do **you** want to share with the world?

LESS IS MORE

When it comes to creating impactful photographs, one of the essential skills to master is the art of balance. However, to achieve balance, **removing unnecessary elements from the photograph** is often necessary rather than adding more.

In photography, balance refers to the **visual harmony** achieved by arranging the different elements in a photograph to create a pleasing and compelling composition. For this, try playing with various elements such as light, colour, texture, shape, and size and finding ways to create a sense of equilibrium between them. The goal behind achieving balance is to guide your viewer's eye through the photograph in a way that allows them to take in all the important details and appreciate the overall aesthetic of the image. So, sometimes, that means taking out all the things that take *away* from these key points you really want them to see.

Less is often more. Instead of adding *more* elements to a photograph, removing any unnecessary elements that might distract from the main subject or detract from the overall composition is often more effective. This is where the art of minimalism comes into play: this way, you can create a clearer and more focused message or mood. This is especially important when it comes to storytelling photography.

In fact, sometimes, if a picture is stripped back to its bare essentials, it creates a more impactful image that is easier for the viewer to engage with. It can also create a sense of calm and simplicity in the image, which is especially effective in creating a mood or emotion in the photograph. This way, the picture can create a sense of space and tranquillity that can appeal to your viewer. This is especially true in landscape photography, where the aim is usually to capture the beauty and serenity of nature.

That being said, it is also tricky to know when to stop removing elements from the photograph. It can be tempting to keep removing elements in the pursuit of simplicity, but there comes a point where removing too much can detract from the overall composition. The key is to find the *right* balance between simplicity and visual interest. This requires careful consideration of the elements in the photograph and how they work together to create a compelling image.

THE ORDINARY

In our lives, we tend to focus on the big moments: graduations, weddings, promotions, and other events that seem significant. But in reality, life is made up of countless small, ordinary moments that are just as important, if not more so. These moments may seem mundane, but they are what truly make up the fabric of our lives. And as photographers, these everyday moments are some of the best opportunities to capture truly incredible images.

People eating, waiting for the bus, hands, gestures, and other small things can be all shards of reality that offer a unique perspective on life. These small moments can capture a moment's essence in a way that larger events cannot. We can create intimate and authentic images focusing on these small details. We can show the world as it is, capturing everyday life's unique beauty.

In fact, these small moments can be opportunities to take great photos. They provide a chance for us to showcase our creativity and unique perspective. A skilled photographer can use these moments to capture images that tell a powerful story, evoke emotion, and inspire others – even if it's a shot as simple as someone in the distance drinking their morning coffee on their way to work. There is beauty in everything, one just needs to *see* it.

For photographers, capturing these little moments is not just about creating a beautiful picture but also about expressing themselves and their unique perspective on the world. Each photographer has a distinctive way of seeing things, and their work is a reflection of their personality, beliefs, and experiences.

For example, Martin Parr's work, a renowned photographer from the United Kingdom, is characterised by his sarcastic point of view on society, particularly in British culture. Through his photography, he portrays the peculiarities and quirks of daily life, from food and fashion to tourism and social habits. Parr's unique approach to photography has made him a celebrated figure in the industry, and his work is often regarded as a commentary on contemporary British society.

The importance of these little moments captured in photography varies depending on your production and approach. Some photographers may focus on capturing the beauty and simplicity of everyday life, while others may highlight society's darker aspects. Regardless of the approach, these moments captured in photography record our experiences, culture, and history. When in a funk, look around you, and try to see the beauty in the mundane.

In fact, you can ask strangers whether you can make their street portrait and can have eye contact. Likewise, objects can tell stories when they are a trace of a person or a story, so do not underestimate them.

Finally, the more confident you feel when leaving your comfort zone, the easier it will be to approach strangers in all kinds of ordinary situations. This is a skill that one needs to develop as a photographer, and taking pictures of people is part of the deal!

LOOK AT THE WHOLE PICTURE

As a photographer, developing **a clear outline of your ideas for small and long-term projects is important.** Taking notes and printing small copies of your photos to see them together can help you refine your vision and stay focused on what you envision for the project you have in mind. Don't only focus on what you need to do next, try to appreciate the present, too!

First, let's consider this: you need to **know yourself**. As a photographer, you have to know who you are so you can have a look at the whole picture. To make sure you can look at the whole picture without getting caught up in the details, you have to know yourself – when do you tend to lose track of the bigger picture? What details often catch your attention, making it difficult for you to stay focused on the bigger picture?

See yourself as an author – there is always a bigger picture, or a bigger goal, behind a book. So, understand what you like, understand the way you see things, and keep this in mind as you photograph either things or people. Your specific perspective is different from anyone else's – you will have your eye on small details that another photographer might see completely differently, so it's up to you to spot this!

Likewise, be persistent. You are a unique photographer with a unique set of skills, so don't give up at the first sight of a challenge. Look at the entire picture, not only the small details that showcase where you may have failed or where something might not have worked out as planned. Keep going and remind yourself why you are interested in photography or in that specific project again. There is always a reason larger than we think! So, outline your ideas, your small and long-term projects, and take notes along the way. You'll be glad to have done so at the end of your project! Speaking concretely about seeing the bigger picture, you should also print small copies of your photos together – this helps you have a better look at what your photo sets look like as a whole, as opposed to only viewing them independently.

Instead of always being focused on what you need to do next, try to enjoy the process and look at other options. For example, use other kinds of media, create AI images to test your creativity, be curious, and feed your imagination, but without focusing on the next project. Try to stay in the present and focus on what you can do *now!* Think about it – when was the last time you discovered something relevant to your creative process?

BREATHE

As a photographer, it's natural to experience moments of disinterest or boredom with your craft. You may feel like you've hit a creative wall or are simply going through the motions without feeling inspired. This is a normal part of the creative process – authors deal with writer's block, and you deal with photographer's block.

When finding your passion again, don't fall into the trap of self-commitments, 365 images per year projects, and social media algorithms. Self-commitments are promises we make to ourselves to do something regularly, which is good in some cases, but it's not efficient if it is not **achievable**. At their best, self-commitments can help us build good habits and achieve our goals. They can give us a sense of accomplishment and help us feel more in control of our lives. However, they can also be harmful if we become too fixated on them. Yes, consistency is important, but taking breaks and giving ourselves time to relax and recharge is okay too, especially when everything feels too overwhelming. We should aim to set realistic goals considering our needs and limitations.

Consistency is important when it comes to pursuing one's passion, but it is not everything. You need a consistent work/life balance – that's what makes a real difference. This means being mindful of your limitations and needs and not pushing yourself too hard or neglecting other aspects of your life, especially when you feel that burnout is incoming.

Let's make something clear, though: I am not saying that you should not have goals, or that having goals is counterproductive. Sometimes, the creative process takes unexpected downturns, but feeling like you are failing to meet your own self-expectations doesn't help either. This is why having a large goal that is barely achievable is not ideal. Instead, try to stick to something you can achieve, and something that will not demotivate you.

Similarly, try not to rush the process. I like to take photos and wait a few days before editing them so that I can take a few days away, breathe, and stop before I jump right into the finishing touches. So, I leave them on purpose to make sure I'll "discover" them again and if I still see myself in them. If not, I know that I need to work on them again, or maybe that I need to discard them altogether. If I *do* still like them, I know that I can keep working on them and that I won't feel like I am wasting my time once I am done with the project.

I also like to go through my archive periodically and see if "something new" pops out to my attention – maybe it's a new project, an important event that needs to be photographed, or something along those lines.

CONCLUSION

"It is putting one's head, one's eye, and one's heart on the same axis."
Henri Cartier-Bresson

Rewriting Henri Cartier-Bresson's quote on the decisive moment, I hope this book will help realign your head with the eye and the heart, in order to see the moments you are sometimes too distracted, overwhelmed or bored to photograph. Sometimes, seeing things differently is really just like seeing them again for the first time.

If you've lost your spark, do not worry – it happens to the best of us. Hopefully, this book was helpful in getting you to find it all over again!

On that note, I wish you the best of luck in your photography endeavours.

Ad maiora semper.
Stefano

A FEW WORDS ABOUT MYSELF

I was born and raised in Italy, where my passion for the visual arts took root. After years of discovery and finding out more about this industry, I then completed an undergraduate degree in Modern Literature, Visual and Performing Arts at the Sapienza University of Rome. This was, without a doubt, an incredible journey! I was able to explore various artistic mediums and develop a strong interest in photography.

I then embarked on a thrilling adventure at the Scuola Romana di Fotografia, again in Italy, where I obtained a Master's Degree in Photography. It was a transformative experience, which not only refined my technical skills but also broadened my perspective through observation and dedication.

Later, in 2011, I was recognised with the first prize in the National Geographic Italy Annual Competition. That same year, Leica Camera Italy acknowledged me as a "Leica Talent", representing the city of Rome in a nationwide photography project.

In 2013, I challenged myself and moved to London, or the European city that never sleeps. This is a choice that has given me the opportunity to share my creative vision with audiences from around the world and meet extraordinary people that taught me the secrets of this profession – one that I find was the right one still to this day!

I now work as Head of Commercial Photography at Global Media and Entertainment, where I have the privilege of translating my artistic vision into captivating visual narratives for various projects. Throughout my journey, although not a straight line so far, I have remained dedicated to the one true passion that likely brought you here.